For Elizabeth Bouton Tether, with love—G.T.
To my mother, a la santé de tes genoux, maman—S.W.

Text copyright © 2005 by Graham Tether. Illustrations copyright © 2005 by
Sylvie Wickstrom. All rights reserved under International and Pan-American
Copyright Conventions. Published in the United States by
Random House Children's Books, a division of Random House, Inc., New York,
and simultaneously in Canada by Random House of Canada Limited, Toronto.

www.randomhouse.com/kids

Library of Congress Cataloging-in-Publication Data
Tether, Graham.
The knee book / by Graham Tether ; illustrated by Sylvie Wickstrom.
p.   cm. — (A bright and early book)
ISBN 0-375-83116-9 (trade) — ISBN 0-375-93116-3 (lib. bdg.)
1. Knee—Juvenile literature.
I. Wickstrom, Sylvie. II. Title. III. Series: Bright & early book.
RD561.T48 2005   617.5'82—dc22
2004028302

Printed in the United States of America   First Edition   10 9 8 7 6 5 4 3 2 1

The KNEE BOOK

By Graham Tether

Illustrated by Sylvie Wickstrom

A Bright and Early Book
From BEGINNER BOOKS®
A Division of Random House, Inc.

KNEES!

KNEES!
They're everywhere!

We see them
here.

We see them
there—

at the circus . . .

at the fair.

We need our knees,
without a doubt!

We need our knees
to walk about . . .

to jump
up high

or crouch
down low.

Nothing works like knees,
you know.

Knees are great
for summer hikes . . .

for jumping rope

and riding bikes.

They help us ski.

They help us skate.

KNEES!

KNEES!

Knees are great!

While upside down
on a flying trapeze,

we'd fall on our heads
without our knees!

We use them each
and every day—

to skip,

to run . . .

to dance,

to play . . .

to mow the lawn,

to pitch the hay.

In summer, when
the weather's hot,

our knees are in
the sun a lot.

When winter comes
and the weather gets breezy,

COVER YOUR KNEES
so they don't get freezy!

So many different
kinds of knees!

Some are fat

and some are thin.

Some bend out

and some bend in . . .

and some are covered
with very thick skin.

Knees are prone
to cuts and scrapes . . .

except if you're one
of those hairy apes!

It's important to remember,
whatever you do,
that knees always come
in sets of two.

Like the wings of a bird
that flies through the air,
knees come together,
two to a pair.

Do fish have knees?
No, none at all . . .

whether they're big
or whether they're small.

No knees on sharks.

No knees on whales.

No knees on dolphins,

worms,

or snails.

If you have knees,
then you're in luck.
Without our knees,
we'd all be stuck!

For every little
move we'd make,
we'd need to slither
like a snake!

I say it once.
I say it twice.
Knees, knees are very nice!

Knees are great
in every way.

Hooray for knees!
Hip, hip, hooray!

Don't take them for granted.
Take good care of them,
please.

And always remember . . .

ENJOY YOUR KNEES!

BRIGHT and EARLY BOOKS for BEGINNING Beginners